The German Shepherd

by William R. Sanford and Carl R. Green

Edited by Julie Bach

CRESTWOOD HOUSE

New York

Collier Macmillan Canada
Toronto

Maxwell Macmillan International Publishing Group
New York   Oxford   Singapore   Sydney

Library of Congress Cataloging-in-Publication Data

Sanford, William R. (William Reynolds), 1927-
   The German shepherd / by William R. Sanford and Carl R. Green ; edited by Julie Bach.
—1st ed.
      p.   cm. — (Top dog series)
   Summary: Discusses the history, physical characteristics, care, and breeding of the
German shepherd.
   ISBN 0-89686-527-4
   1. German shepherd dogs—Juvenile literature.   [1. German shepherd dogs.   2. Dogs.]
I. Green, Carl R.   II. Bach, Julie S., 1963-   III. Title.   IV. Series: Top dog
(Crestwood House)
SF429.G37S26   1990
636.7′37—dc20   90-34212
                                                                                 CIP
                                                                                 AC

PHOTO CREDITS

Cover: Elizabeth Fox / Simba and Bear, owned and
   trained by James Kough
Kent and Donna Dannen: 4, 6, 15, 19, 22, 37, 39, 43
Elizabeth Fox: 9, 20, 25, 29, 44
Jeff Lampke: 11, 16, 33, 40
Chandoha Photography: (Walter Chandoha) 26

CRESTWOOD HOUSE

Macmillan Publishing Company
866 Third Avenue
New York, NY 10022

Collier Macmillan Canada, Inc.
1200 Eglinton Avenue East
Suite 200
Don Mills, Ontario M3C 3N1

Printed in the United States of America

First Edition

10   9   8   7   6   5   4   3   2   1

◣CONTENTS

A Lifesaving Friend 5

The History of a Useful Breed 7

The German Shepherd in Close-Up 10

A Working Dog's Keen Senses 14

A Dog with Personality 18

Choosing a German Shepherd Puppy 21

Training a German Shepherd 24

Caring for Your German Shepherd 28

Breeding a Female German Shepherd 31

The Miracle of Birth......................34

German Shepherds in Competition 36

Talented Herders 38

Joining the Police Force 42

Glossary/Index 46–48

For more information about German shepherds, write to:

German Shepherd Club of America
17 West Ivy Lane
Englewood, NJ 07631

Schutzhund USA
c/o Sara Hitchens
2 Sierra Morena
Woodside, CA 94062

A LIFESAVING FRIEND

Morris Frank was upset. He was due to speak at a meeting in minutes, but his train had arrived late and he still had to go to his hotel to change. He reached his room on the fourteenth floor and quickly put on a clean shirt. He wondered if he'd make it to the meeting on time.

Five minutes later, Morris was hurrying down the hallway. His blindness didn't slow his steps. His big German shepherd, Buddy, led the way. Buddy was Morris's *Seeing Eye* dog.

To Morris's surprise, Buddy stopped before he reached the elevator. Morris urged him forward, but the dog refused to move. Buddy was supposed to point to the call button with his nose. Why was he holding back?

Morris then did what Seeing Eye owners are told never to do. He dropped the harness and walked forward on his own. Instantly, Buddy threw himself against his owner's legs. Try as he might, Morris couldn't push past the dog.

At that moment, a maid came out of a room down the hall. She took one look and yelled, "Don't move! If you step forward, you'll fall down the elevator shaft."

German shepherds have been trained to herd sheep, help police, and act as Seeing Eye dogs.

Morris felt faint. If Buddy hadn't stopped him, he would have walked through the open door and plunged to his death. The Seeing Eye dog had saved his life.

Buddy had been Morris's guide dog since 1927. That year, Morris had heard that Europeans were training dogs to guide blind people. He went to Switzerland where he and Buddy were trained to work together. When they returned to the United States, they caused quite a stir. Buddy was America's first Seeing Eye dog.

The training needed to become a good Seeing Eye dog begins when a shepherd is still a puppy.

After his close call at the elevator, Morris felt closer than ever to Buddy. The German shepherd had already helped him gain his independence. Now he had saved Morris's life as well.

THE HISTORY OF A USEFUL BREED

All domestic dogs belong to the *species* scientists call *Canis familiaris*. They were tamed by humans long ago to hunt food and guard against enemies at night. Later, dogs also learned to herd sheep, goats, and cattle. They helped their owners move large groups of these animals from one grazing ground to another.

In Germany, herders used the best dogs they could find. They didn't care what the dogs looked like. But in the 1890s, a man named Captain Max von Stephanitz started a club called the Verein. The members of this club wanted to establish a special German herding dog. They chose top dogs and mated them.

Soon a new *breed* emerged from the varied shepherd dogs of Germany. The German shepherd was the result of the Verein's careful *breeding*.

German shepherds were first brought to the United States in 1906. The breed was accepted by the American Kennel Club (AKC) six years later. German shepherds had been bred as sheepdogs, but the dogs proved to be good at almost everything. Some won ribbons in shows. Others served with the police and the military. Proud owners of these talented dogs formed the German Shepherd Dog Club in 1913.

During World War I, when the United States was at war with Germany, many Americans didn't like anything associated with their enemies. Suddenly, German shepherds were no longer such popular dogs. To save the breed, the AKC changed its name to "shepherd dog." Fortunately, when the war ended, German shepherds came into favor again. Soldiers even brought some home from Europe. The name wasn't changed back to German shepherd, however, until 1931.

During the 1920s, two German shepherds became famous. Strongheart and Rin Tin Tin starred in a number of silent movies. Film critics even said that "Rinty" was a better actor than his human co-stars. The original Rin Tin

Because they are brave and have keen senses, German shepherds were used in the U.S. Army's K-9 Corps during World War II.

Tin died in 1932, but other shepherds played his part and kept his fame alive. The last Rin Tin Tin was retired after appearing in a 1950s television serial. Thanks to these two film stars, the demand for German shepherds grew. Breeders were soon producing 25,000 puppies a year.

During World War II, German shepherds were drafted into the U.S. Army. They were one of the few breeds accepted in the army's *K-9 Corps*. These fearless dogs served as sentries and were often used to sniff out hidden enemy

9

soldiers. When called on, the dogs also carried medicines and supplies through thick jungles.

Today, the German shepherd still ranks in the top ten of America's dogs. Its strength, good looks, and quick wits have earned the dog that honor many times over.

THE GERMAN SHEPHERD IN CLOSE-UP

German shepherds are strong, noble dogs. They are large and muscular, but they are also graceful and controlled. They have been bred for both beauty and hard work.

Adult males are 25 inches tall at the *withers*. They measure about 30 inches from chest to rump. Males weigh between 75 and 85 pounds. Adult females are about 23 inches tall at the withers. From chest to rump they are about 27 inches long. They weigh between 60 and 70 pounds.

All German shepherds have double coats to keep them warm, left from the days when they were herding sheep in northern Europe. The

10

An adult male German shepherd can weigh between 75 and 85 pounds.

medium-length hair of these dense outer coats is straight and lies close to the body. The wiry undercoat keeps water and cold from reaching the skin. Shepherds' coats can be many different colors, but they are usually shades of brown and black. German shepherds that are entered in dog shows are not supposed to have white patches.

The German shepherd's head is well shaped. Its muzzle is a long wedge, the lips are firm, and the nose is black. The shepherd's large, slightly pointed ears are turned forward and stand proudly erect. Its almond-shaped eyes are alert and dark. The well-trained shepherd seems to look at the world with quiet dignity.

At five months, a shepherd's baby teeth are replaced by 42 adult teeth. The 4 sharp *canines* are for ripping a good-sized piece of meat. The 12 *incisors* are for biting. The *molars* and *premolars* are for chewing, but a dog doesn't have to chew the way a human does. Its stomach easily digests large pieces of food.

A German shepherd's front teeth overlap in a scissors bite. Its powerful jaw muscles can exert 750 pounds of pressure when they snap shut. That's enough force to crush a burglar's forearm. The strength of a shepherd's jaw is one reason some people are afraid of the breed.

The lines of a shepherd's body are smoothly flowing curves. Its chest is deep and its abdomen firm. The ribs are widely spaced, allowing room for a large heart and strong lungs. A relaxed shepherd holds its head and neck slightly above shoulder level. An alert or excited dog raises its head for a better look around. Its long, muscular neck lacks the loose folds of skin seen in other breeds.

The shepherd's forelegs are straight, and its hindlegs are angled for leverage and power. The high withers slope down from the neck to the rump. The back is straight, without sag or sway. The shepherd's bushy, slightly curved tail hangs down when the dog is at rest. The tail should be long enough to reach the lower joint in the hind leg. A shepherd with a *docked*, or shortened, tail cannot compete in AKC shows.

A German shepherd moves with a graceful, flowing gait. Even at a slow walk, the dog's long stride covers ground quickly. In a trot, the stride lengthens. When a shepherd shifts gears for a high-speed gallop, very few animals can outrun it.

A WORKING DOG'S KEEN SENSES

Owners of German shepherds are certain that their dogs are brighter than most other breeds. But they know, of course, that their dogs aren't as smart as humans. The shepherd's three-ounce brain is tiny compared to a human's three-pound brain. A brain that small can't think like a human brain can.

Dogs can learn to respond to certain commands, but the words themselves mean nothing to them. Say "Hugger!" every time you speak to your dog, and it will soon answer to that name. Not even the brightest German shepherd can solve simple problems. In one test, a hungry dog was placed in a "puzzle box." A dish of meat was waiting outside the bars of the box. To get to the meat, the dog had to pull on a ring that dangled from the lid of the box. The dog barked and pawed at the bars and finally pulled the ring by accident. But when placed in the box a second time, the dog couldn't remember that the ring would release it. Cats, on the other hand, can learn to pull the ring to free themselves. Dogs always seem confused by the problem.

In spite of their lack of intelligence, dogs are still able to do many things. Their *instincts* and keen senses make them "smart" in a different way than people are. For example, dogs have extremely keen senses of hearing and smell.

German shepherds can hear fainter sounds and can locate their source better than we can. They also hear sounds that are too high-pitched for humans to hear. Human hearing

A German shepherd can use its sharp sense of smell to find people who have gotten lost in the woods.

stops with sounds that measure about 20,000 cycles a second. That's why dogs come running when you blow on a "silent" dog whistle. They can hear the whistle's 30,000-cycle sound when you can't.

A German shepherd's sense of smell is even more amazing. A shepherd's nose picks up scents that a human's nose could never detect. Much of the dog's brain is used to make sense out of the data that comes in from the nose. That's why German shepherds can sniff out objects and people that humans would overlook. Police in Birmingham, Alabama, confirmed that fact. After they had twice failed to find a burglar who had hidden in a warehouse, they brought in a police dog. The shepherd found the man in less than five minutes.

The German shepherd's eyesight is much weaker than its hearing and sense of smell. Like all dogs, shepherds are color-blind and their distance vision is poor. They do have a wide field of vision, though, and they're highly sensitive to movement. These traits probably are inherited from the dog's wild ancestors. Wild dogs may go hungry if they can't spot movements made by their prey. Dogs also have a third eyelid called a *haw*. It cleans and protects the eyeball.

With careful training, a shepherd can be taught to sniff out objects hidden in fields. It can use this skill to help policemen locate drugs and people.

A DOG WITH PERSONALITY

Year after year, German shepherds remain one of the most popular of all dogs. The reason is simple. No other dog can do so many things so well.

The same German shepherd can be a pet, a show dog, and a watchdog. With a little extra training, it can also become a police dog or a *guard dog*. German shepherds serve as Seeing Eye dogs, attack dogs, and as members of search-and-rescue teams. The shepherd that stars in movies can also herd sheep.

The breed standards developed in Germany describe the shepherd as calm, alert, courageous, and loyal. If the job calls for it, the shepherd can be trained to display an aggressive but controlled fighting spirit. These traits are the result of more than 80 years of careful breeding. Dull, vicious, or timid shepherds have been weeded out.

The German shepherd's ability to be aggressive frightens many people. But owners of shepherds swear that their dogs are not dangerous brutes. It is true that they can pin down a fleeing criminal or attack a burglar, but they also can be very friendly. They can play

German shepherds are friendly dogs that make good companions for children.

gently with children and make friends with anyone their owners tell them is okay.

The German Shepherd Club of America uses a test to measure each dog's personality. The seven-part test grades the dog on its reactions to strangers, sudden noises, and other threats. A shepherd that passes the test earns a *Temperament Certificate.*

Perhaps shepherds trained for search-and-rescue work best show the breed's talents. These dogs have fine noses and rock-solid nerves. They learn to climb ladders, ride in helicopters, and move quickly across rough ground. When shepherds find someone buried in the snow, they signal their handlers. Then they begin digging to free the victim.

As marvelous as German shepherds are, they're not for everyone. Unless they're trained as Seeing Eye dogs, they're too big for tiny apartments. They need daily exercise, and their thick coat requires regular *grooming*. In addition, these people-loving dogs can become difficult to handle if they're left alone too often. There's also the dog's appetite to consider. It takes a lot of food to keep a shepherd healthy.

Adult German shepherds need plenty of exercise and careful grooming.

CHOOSING A GERMAN SHEPHERD PUPPY

So, you and your family are going to buy a German shepherd puppy! That's great news. But before you go shopping, ask yourself a few questions.

Is my home ready for a puppy? Most people know that a puppy needs a bed, food, and toys. They forget that a puppy also needs security. You need a place to keep the dog when you're not home. Inside the house, a playpen or large crate will do the job. If you have a yard, it will need a strong fence. Puppies that run loose are a danger to themselves and to others.

Should I buy from a pet store or a breeder? If you have a choice, buy from a breeder who can show you one or more *litters* of puppies. The pet store may be closer, but it will probably have only one puppy on hand. At a kennel you can also see the puppy's mother. Your puppy will probably look like her when it's grown.

A shepherd puppy as playful and healthy as this one will probably grow up to be a good pet.

Your local *veterinarian* can give you a list of quality breeders and pet stores.

How do I know the puppy is healthy? Healthy puppies are playful and clean. Watch out for puppies that have cloudy eyes, swollen bellies, or runny noses. Check the puppy for deafness by snapping your fingers behind its head. Have the puppies had their shots? The seller should be able to show you a complete health record. When you do choose a puppy, take it to your vet as soon as possible for a checkup.

How much will the puppy cost? If you want a blue-ribbon *show dog*, expect to pay $750 or more. (A Japanese breeder paid a record $300,000 for a champion stud male!) A pet-quality dog that has all the shepherd's fine qualities will cost around $350. A pet-quality dog can be trained for any task you have in mind. It lacks only the perfect form that wins dog shows.

Is buying a purebred dog important? A *purebred* shepherd has the qualities of its breed. A mixed-breed puppy may grow up to be a fine dog, or it may turn out badly. You won't know at the time you buy it because it is difficult to say for sure what breeds it comes from or how the breeds will mix. When you buy a purebred, the breeder will give you a *pedigree* that lists the puppy's ancestors. These papers also allow you to register the dog with one of the national kennel clubs.

Do I want a male or female puppy? Both males and females make good pets. Males are more likely to roam, but females go into *heat* twice a year. That's when the female is ready to mate and have puppies. You'll have to keep male dogs away from her during this time.

How old should a puppy be when it leaves its litter? A German shepherd puppy can go home with you when it is eight to ten weeks old. That's when the fun and hard work of training begin.

TRAINING A GERMAN SHEPHERD

A German shepherd puppy comes with the instincts of a wild pack animal. If it's not trained, it will cause endless problems. Luckily, there's nothing mysterious about dog training. Patience and firmness are the only tools one needs.

German shepherds are naturally clean, so it is easy to *housebreak* them. After the dog eats or wakes up from a nap, take it outside or to the spot you want it to use to relieve itself. Say "Good dog" when it performs properly. The scent the dog leaves there will encourage it to use the same spot again. Don't punish the puppy when it has an accident. Clean up the mess and go on with your training.

Your puppy will develop some bad habits if you don't train it early. For example, it

Teaching your German shepherd to sit and stay on command is very important. Shepherds learn quickly and will soon follow your commands.

probably will try to chew everything in sight, including your hands and ankles. This play-biting may seem cute, but you can't let it continue. When your dog bites, pinch its cheek lightly. This is the way a mother dog corrects a pup that bites her. Say "No! No biting!" at the same time. One cheek pinch will probably be enough. A puppy soon learns to respect the person who corrects its behavior.

Your dog may also like to jump up on people. That's okay when it's a puppy, but a full-grown shepherd can knock people down when it jumps on them. When your dog tries to jump on you, throw it off balance with your knee. Say "No jumping!" in a firm voice. After it settles down, kneel and pet it while you say "Good dog!"

If you teach your puppy some simple commands, such as "sit," "lie down," and "stay," you'll be able to control it. To teach your puppy to sit, stand in front of it and hold out your hand, palm down. Say "Sit!" Push down on its hips if you have to. To make it lie down, pull it down with a leash. Once it's sitting or lying, say "Stay!" Reward good behavior with praise and a bit of dog biscuit.

You might also want to train your dog to ride in a car. Shepherds usually don't get carsick, but take a towel with you just in case. It is okay

Rewarding puppies with treats when they learn something new will help them follow commands more quickly.

to let your dog cuddle next to you for security, but don't let it roam around. If it tries to move from one window to another, say "No. Sit!" Repeat these lessons as often as they're needed.

Puppies usually cry when they're left alone. To teach your dog not to cry, put it in a room with toys and a bowl of water. Tell it "Wait!" as you leave and close the door. If it cries, return and repeat the command. After several tries, your dog will allow you to leave for a short time. When you return, reward the good behavior with praise and a doggy treat. Your puppy will soon learn that being left alone isn't forever.

CARING FOR YOUR GERMAN SHEPHERD

German shepherds are strong, vigorous dogs. But that doesn't mean they can be neglected. A shepherd needs a proper diet, a warm sleeping place, grooming and exercise, and trips to the vet.

Good care begins with a well-balanced diet.

With lots of attention, good training, and proper feeding, German shepherds can be wonderful pets.

The puppy foods sold in stores are easy to use, but you can also mix your own puppy diet. A basic mix contains raw chopped beef, wheat germ, a cooked egg, and a bonemeal tablet. Blend the dry foods into a formula of canned milk, water, and Karo syrup.

An eight-week-old puppy needs five small meals a day. As it grows, it will eat larger and fewer meals. A four-month-old needs only three meals a day, and a nine-month-old needs only two. A one-year-old will do well on a 24-ounce evening meal of raw meat and cereals.

Make sure you never feed your dog from the table. This can lead to begging and a taste for sweets. Also, never give your dog fish or chicken bones. These bones can splinter and stick in the dog's throat. Throw it some soft beef rib bones instead. These bones clean your dog's teeth as it chews on them. Experts call them "the dog's toothbrush."

Despite their size, German shepherds are easy to house. A dog that sleeps inside needs only a box lined with newspapers and a piece of blanket. An outdoor dog needs a sturdy doghouse. A large barrel set up on cement blocks will do. Even the most costly doghouse is a poor choice if the floor touches the ground. A dog whose bed is damp and cold is almost certain to become ill.

Shepherds love to be groomed. If you can't brush the dog every day, do so at least twice a week. Grooming keeps the coat sleek, tones the skin, and cuts down on *shedding*. Shepherds don't need to be clipped like poodles and other breeds. They do need to have their toenails trimmed and their ears wiped out. Shampoos, powders, and a flea collar will protect the dog from fleas.

A well-cared-for German shepherd will live between 12 and 14 years. To reach this age, a dog needs sunshine, exercise, and visits to the vet. An outdoor dog run will take care of the sunshine, but exercise is up to you. Left alone, shepherds tend to become "couch potatoes." A fast daily walk and a game of fetch will keep the dog's muscles firm and its weight down. Take your dog to the vet regularly. The vet will give your dog its shots and check it for *worms*.

BREEDING A FEMALE GERMAN SHEPHERD

Because the puppies inherit their parents' strengths and weaknesses, people try to plan each breeding with great care. They never breed a female, or *bitch*, with physical defects or behavior problems. They select *studs* with equal care.

Breeders also try to be sure their dogs don't have *hip dysplasia*, a disease common to large dogs. Dysplasia cripples a dog; dysplastic shepherds must be put to sleep. If both parents of a litter have bad hips, more than 90 percent of the puppies will inherit the condition. If only one parent is dysplastic, about 50 percent of the puppies will be affected. If neither parent is dysplastic, fewer than 10 percent will have bad hips.

Of course, you don't have to breed your female German shepherd. Your veterinarian can *spay* her. This simple operation prevents your dog from ever getting pregnant. It costs about $100. You can also make sure your male dog doesn't make a female dog pregnant. Your vet can *neuter* him. That operation costs about the same as spaying.

If you decide to breed your female shepherd, the dog should first be checked by a vet. She can be bred from her second heat until she's about four years old. The stud's owner will have you bring her to the kennels between the 12th and 14th days of her heat. If she's ready to mate, she'll let the stud approach her without protest. Afterward, take her for a fast walk. If the timing was good, a pregnancy will result. If nothing happens, the stud's owner will schedule another try.

The dog will then need some special attention. First, she must be kept away from other males until her heat is over. A second mating with a male of another breed could result in a mixed litter. Second, she must be taken back to the vet. The vet can confirm the pregnancy and suggest ways to care for her. She may need

A German shepherd puppy needs to stay with its mother until it is eight weeks old.

more protein in her diet, for example. Feeding her raw liver in the last month will help her produce milk for the puppies. Exercise is also important. A dog will have an easier delivery if she's in good shape.

Prepare a *whelping box* in the seventh week of your dog's pregnancy. A German shepherd needs a large box about two feet high by five feet square. The best box has a four-inch guard rail along the sides. The rail keeps the dog from crushing newborn puppies that crawl behind her. A wooden step will make it easier for her to climb in and out. After the box is lined with newspaper and straw, give her time to get used to it. She'll soon hollow out a nest in the straw.

There's not much else to do after the dog accepts the whelping box. Her instincts will guide her when the births begin.

THE MIRACLE OF BIRTH

Like all dogs, a German shepherd bitch carries her puppies for nine weeks. If the litter is a large one, you'll see her abdomen expand after the fifth week. By the ninth week she'll be restless. She may refuse food, and she'll scratch at the lining of the whelping box.

Birth begins with a series of contractions in the mother's abdomen. Most newborn puppies emerge head first, but tail-first births are also common. Each *whelp* is born in a birth sac, which the mother removes with her teeth. Then the mother bites off the *umbilical cord* and licks the puppy clean. The action of her rough tongue encourages the puppy to take its first breaths. If a whelp still needs cleaning, you can wipe it with a warm, damp cloth, then dry it gently with a towel.

A new whelp will appear every 30 minutes or so. Consult a vet if the mother is having a hard labor. A shot can help ease the delivery. After the birth of its last whelp, the mother dog will nudge the deaf and blind whelps into position to begin nursing. They'll begin sucking when their mouths touch the *teats*. Take your dog out for a run after she's nursed the puppies for a while. Then encourage her to eat some dog meal soaked in milk.

After three days, a vet should give the pups a checkup. This is a good time to have the useless *dewclaws* removed from their hind legs. The vet will also examine the mother. Nursing females can develop illnesses caused by poor diet or infections.

From this point on, the puppies will grow quickly. Their eyes will open at ten days, and they'll become more active. Clip their toenails to keep them from scratching each other. At three weeks, you can give them their first taste of lean chopped beef. This is the first step in *weaning* them from their mother. Within another week, they should be drinking cow's milk from a dish. By four weeks, their mother will be nursing the puppies only at night. By then they will also need their first puppy shots.

The busy weeks will speed by. Suddenly the fast-growing puppies will be eight weeks old— old enough to be taken to new homes.

GERMAN SHEPHERDS IN COMPETITION

Take your young and eager German shepherd for a walk in the park. Some people will give you extra room when you and your dog pass by. Others are likely to ask, "Is it trained for competition?"

German shepherds are successful competitors. Some shepherds are entered in shows in which they're judged strictly on their looks. Other shepherds are trained for *obedience trials* or sheepherding trials. In a typical obedience trial, the dog must obey all commands instantly. It must perform as well without a leash as with one. These tests are based strictly on what a dog can do, not on how it looks.

If a dog succeeds in the first level of obedience trials, it earns the title of Companion Dog (CD). If it succeeds in more difficult tests, it earns the rank of Companion Dog Excellent (CDX). The best CDX dogs are tested for the highest level, that of Utility Dog (UD). In this series of tests, the dog must obey voice and hand commands instantly. It must also follow a scent, retrieve objects, and jump obstacles.

In the major leagues of obedience trials, dogs can earn the top title of *Schutzhund*. The German word means "guard dog," but a *Schutzhund* can do much more than simply guard a home. These finely trained shepherds excel in obedience, tracking, and protection. They can follow unmarked trails, find hidden objects, and clear a jump 39 inches high. When it's on duty, a *Schutzhund* can use just its teeth

In a high-level obedience trial, a shepherd has to clear jumps and find hidden objects.

to subdue an intruder. Away from home, the dog attacks only when its owner gives the command.

Dog competitions are tough for both dogs and their owners. A shepherd's owner must groom it perfectly and show it expertly. The dog must allow strangers to handle it without protest. At obedience trials, the dog must show a high degree of control. In one *Schutzhund* test, for example, a judge fires a gun while the dog is off the leash. A dog that shies away from the noise fails the trial.

Owners who enter their dogs in competition are proud of their awards. They agree, however, that it's not the cups and ribbons that inspire them. The real thrill lies in watching their beautiful shepherds perform.

TALENTED HERDERS

Watching a German shepherd herd sheep can be fascinating. The dog circles at top speed, keeping the sheep together. The dog doesn't bark or snap at the noisy flock. But if a sheep starts to stray, the dog will be there

The German shepherd has natural herding instincts inherited from its wolf ancestors.

instantly to head it off. It's as though the shepherd is reading the mind of the sheep and the human sheepherder.

The German shepherd inherits its herding instincts from its wolf ancestors. Modern wolves still show these behaviors. When a wolf pack sights a caribou herd, it spreads out and encircles the herd. As the wolves close in, they stay an equal distance from each other. If a caribou tries to break free, the nearest wolves drive it back. Each wolf obeys signals from the pack leader all through the hunt.

The wolves' hunting behaviors were passed down to shepherd dogs. Watch a shepherd at work. The first thing you notice is that the dog seems to be everywhere at once. First it runs to a spot near the flock and crouches there. Then it's off and running to another spot. A voice calls out an order, and the dog turns the flock toward an uphill pasture. This one dog is doing the work of an entire pack! It's also accepting commands from the pack leader—the human sheepherder.

Herding sheep is tiring. These dogs take a rest and cool off.

A German shepherd needs only ten commands to herd sheep. The sheepherder gives the commands by voice, by whistling, or by hand movements. Here's what they mean to the dog:

Stop! Whatever you're doing now, quit.

Come in! Move closer to the sheep.

Get back! Move away from the sheep.

Go left! Move to the left of the sheep. If the signal is repeated: Keep circling to the left.

Go right! Move to the right of the sheep. If the signal is repeated: Keep circling to the right.

Come here! Move toward the sheepherder.

Lie down! Stop where you are and face the sheep. Crouch down and stare at them.

Speed up! Continue the movement but do it faster.

Steady! Continue the movement but do it slower.

That will do! Move to the sheepherder's side.

These commands allow a sheepherder to control a restless flock with only a single dog. Most of the movements are natural to German shepherds. Only those commands that ask the dogs to move away from the sheep go against their instincts. That's where training takes over. The canine shepherds obey instantly, no matter what the command.

JOINING THE POLICE FORCE

The city of Philadelphia was suffering from a long series of purse snatchings. The thieves often struck while their victims were crossing a supermarket parking lot. Some elderly women had been badly hurt. The police had to do something.

Officers dressed as older women were sent to walk the troubled streets. The decoys carried groceries and let their purses dangle from their shoulders. An unmarked patrol car followed them. When a purse snatcher struck, the patrol car door flew open and a German shepherd bounded out. The dog ran down the frightened thief and pulled him to the ground. Moments later, the officers ran up to make the easy arrest.

The dog patrols were a great success. In just a few weeks, one team made 12 arrests. That brought the purse snatching to an end. No one wanted to risk being caught in the strong jaws of a police dog.

Today, more than 90 percent of the nation's thousands of K-9 dogs are German shepherds. These dogs help police forces protect the

Police often use German shepherds to track down suspected criminals and sniff out illegal drugs.

public. Sending K-9 patrols into an area often reduces the crime rate overnight. In addition, it costs less to buy and train dogs than to hire more officers.

Fleeing suspects are more likely to stop for a dog than for an armed officer. In Baltimore a prowler jumped from the second floor of a warehouse when he saw a police dog closing in. He told the arresting officers that the sight of the dog's open jaws was scarier than jumping. In ten months, Baltimore's 15-dog K-9 unit made 175 arrests!

Most police forces assign a police officer and a dog to a squad car. During their patrols, the officers release the shepherds whenever they see something suspicious. The dog is trained to approach and bark at suspects who don't run. Those who do run are quickly chased down. The chase almost always ends with the dog grabbing the suspects by the arm. Then the dog holds them until help arrives.

Police dogs are usually trained by their human partners. The dogs live at the officers' homes. Although they make gentle pets, police dogs will attack anyone who threatens their trainer's family. That's why the police warn against giving attack training to pet dogs. A child could easily become angry at a playmate and give the attack command. Or a neighbor could chase a ball into a yard where a dog is kept. The result in either case could be tragic.

Patrolling the streets isn't the only job assigned to police dogs. K-9 teams control crowds and guard jails. The dogs are also good at sniffing out hidden drugs and bombs. One German shepherd found $3.5 million worth of marijuana hidden in a truckload of onions! The shepherd's trainer wasn't surprised. Amazing feats like that are all in a day's work for a German shepherd.

The well-trained shepherd seems to look at the world with quiet dignity.

GLOSSARY/ INDEX

Bitch 31, 34—An adult female dog.

Breed 8, 12, 13, 14, 18, 19, 31, 34—A particular type of dog with common ancestors and similar characteristics. The German shepherd is one breed of dog.

Breeding 8, 31—Mating a quality female to a quality male.

Canines 12—The four long, sharp holding teeth in the front of a dog's mouth.

Dewclaws 35—Extra, useless claws that grow on the insides of a dog's legs. These are removed at birth by a vet.

Docked 13—A dog's tail shortened by cutting it off at the first or second joint.

Grooming 20, 30, 38—Bathing and brushing a dog to keep its coat clean and smooth.

Guard Dog 18, 37—A dog that's been trained to protect people and property.

Haw 17—An extra eyelid that helps protect a dog's eye.

Heat 23—The days when a bitch is ready to mate.

Hip Dysplasia 31, 32—An inherited condition that affects a dog's hip joints. A severe case can cripple a German shepherd.

Housebreak 24—To train a puppy to relieve itself on newspaper or outside the house.

Incisors 12—The nipping and cutting teeth between the canines.

Instincts 15, 24, 39—Natural behaviors that are inborn in a dog.

K-9 Corps 9, 42, 43, 45—Dogs trained for police or military work.

Litter 21, 23, 31, 32—A family of puppies born at a single whelping.

Molars 12—A dog's back teeth, used for chewing and grinding.

Neuter 32—To operate on a male dog so he can't make a female dog pregnant.

Obedience Trial 36, 37, 38—A competition in which dogs are judged on how well they obey a series of commands.

Pedigree 23—A chart that lists a dog's ancestors.

Premolars 12—A dog's teeth located in front of the molars. They are used for chewing and grinding.

Purebred 23—A dog whose ancestors were all of the same breed.

Schutzhund 37, 38—A highly trained guard dog. A German shepherd earns this ranking by passing a series of demanding obedience, tracking, and protection tests.

Seeing Eye 5, 6, 18, 20—A dog specially trained to lead the blind.

Shedding 30—Losing hair.

Show Dog 23—A dog that meets the highest standards of its breed.

Spay 32—To remove a female dog's ovaries so she can't become pregnant.

Species 7—A group of animals or plants with common and distinctive features.

Stud 31, 32—A purebred male used for breeding.

Teats 35—A female dog's nipples. Puppies suck on the teats to get milk.

Temperament Certificate (TC) 18—A rating earned by German shepherds that have proven their ability to remain calm in almost any situation.

Umbilical Cord 34—A hollow tube that carries nutrients to a puppy while it is in its mother's body.

Veterinarian 22, 23, 28, 30, 31, 32, 35—A doctor trained to take care of animals

Weaning 35—Making a puppy stop drinking its mother's milk and eat solid food instead.

Whelp 34, 35—A puppy; a dog under one year of age.

Whelping Box 33, 34—A box in which a female dog can give birth to her puppies.

Withers 10—A dog's shoulders; the point where its neck joins the body. A dog's height is measured at the withers.

Worms 31—Parasites that live in a dog's intestines and can make it sick.